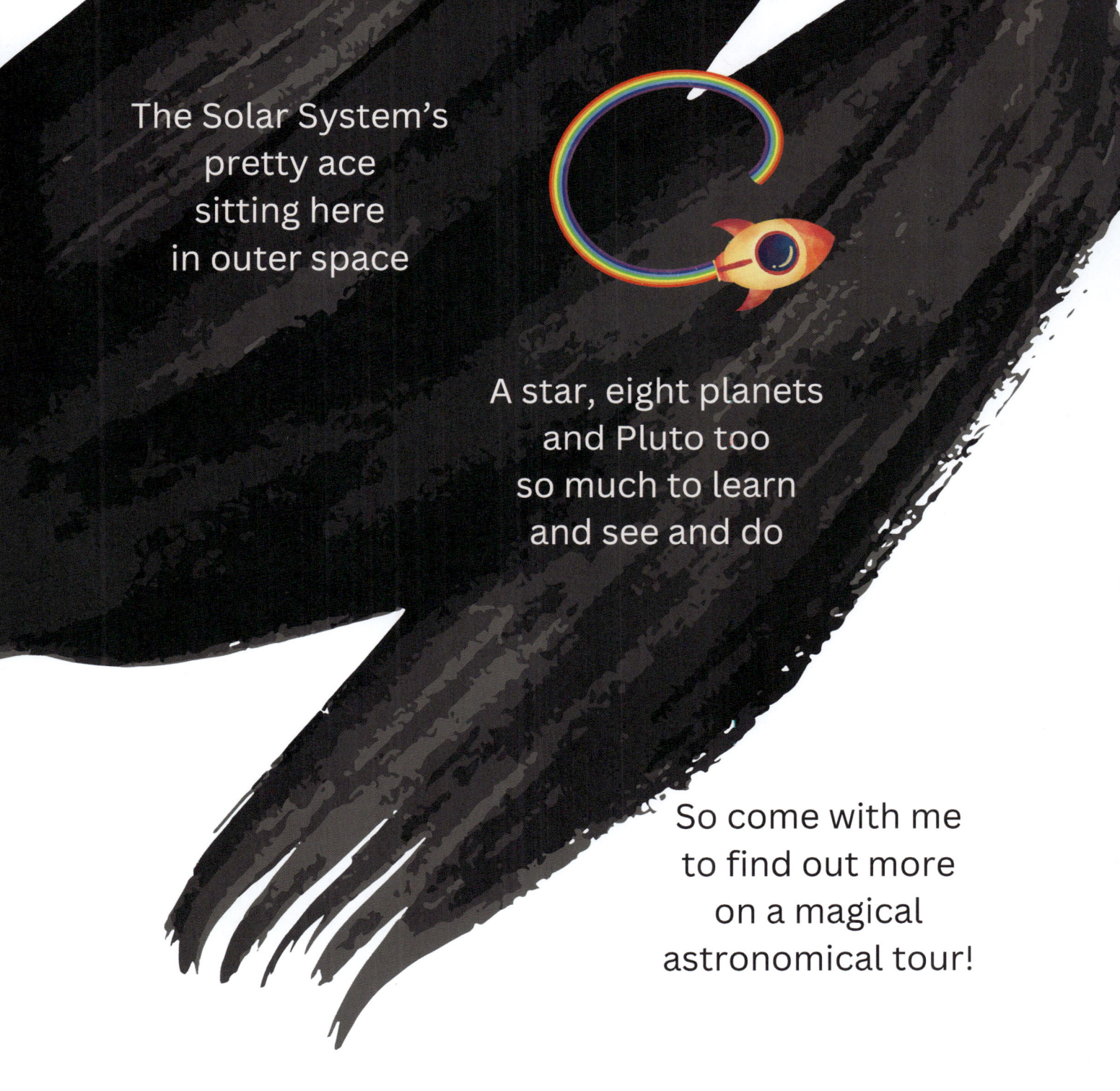

The Solar System's
pretty ace
sitting here
in outer space

A star, eight planets
and Pluto too
so much to learn
and see and do

So come with me
to find out more
on a magical
astronomical tour!

The Sun is huge
and rather neat
a natural source
of light and heat!

Mercury's closest
to the sun
its speedy orbit's
really fun!

Venus is hot
and thick with cloud
it shines so bright
so very proud

Earth is our home
it's where we live
so full of life
so much to give!

Mars might look warm
but don't be fooled
this small red ball
is rather cold

Here's Jupiter
a big gas ball
the biggest planet
of them all!

Saturn's majestic
wrapped in rings
made of ice and rock
and other things

Uranus has
a crazy orbit
it's on its side
you can't ignore it!

Neptune is blue
an icy place
the coldest planet
in outer space

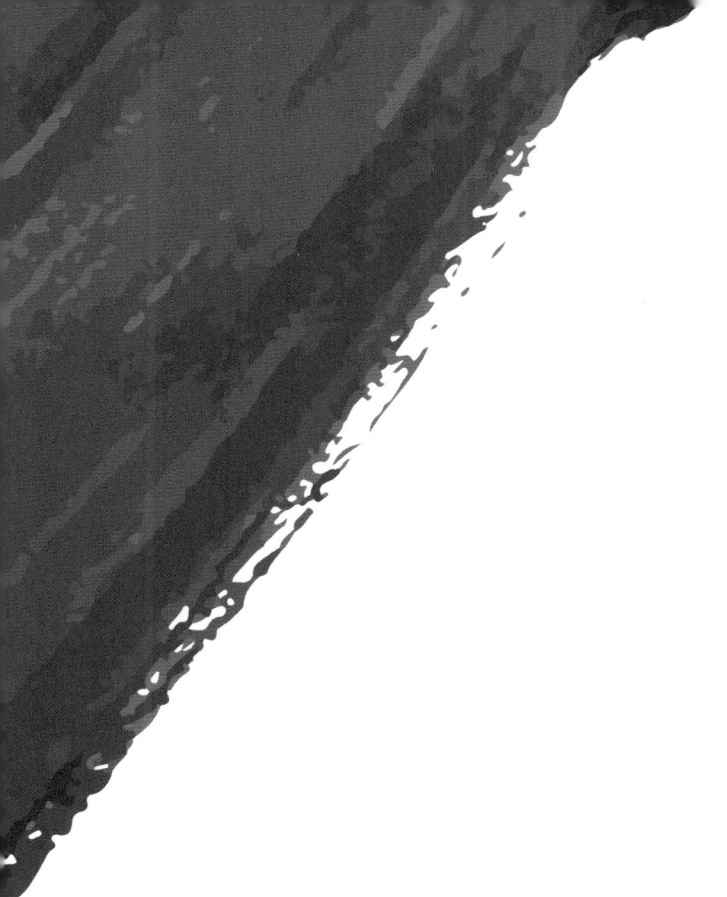

Pluto's not a planet
but we don't mind
this tiny rock
is one of a kind!

So now you know
a little bit
about the Solar System
and what's in it

But there's more to learn
so don't stop here
go out, explore
and have no fear!

Printed in Great Britain
by Amazon